The Smart Mom's Guide to Starting Solids
How to Introduce, Advance & Nourish Your Baby with First Foods
(& Avoid the Most Common Mistakes)
By Jill Castle, MS, RDN

Contents

Introduction

I had my first baby in 1996. In the next five years, I would add three more babies to the family. You could say that I did some intensive baby feeding during that time of my life as a mom.

Several things became clear to me. Every baby is different—even within families. Their food preferences evolve differently, the way they experience food is individualized, and they can progress at a different pace from one another.

I also made mistakes. My first child became iron deficient at 18 months. And, she grew on the low end of the growth curve (a hard pill to swallow as a dietitian!). My last baby developed food allergies at age two.

You could say I cut my food parenting teeth on my first child, like many parents do. Back then, the nutrition resources for feeding your baby were slim and hard to find.

Being a pediatric dietitian helped quite a bit, but it certainly didn't prevent me from the struggles, doubt and guilt that nagged at my conscience during those early years.

Are my kids healthy today? I believe so. My first baby is now a young adult and no longer iron deficient nor underweight. My last baby is a teenager and still manages a food allergen free diet. They are healthy today, in part, because I corrected my food and feeding mistakes.

Today, parents like you have many more resources from which to draw information about feeding your baby. That's a good thing...and that can be a bad thing. One thing is certain, the world of baby food has changed.

The days of glass jars and plain rice cereal, though still here, are fading to a world of whole foods, self-feeding, convenient packaging, and unique flavor blends. Baby food has been remodeled and revitalized, and will never be the same.

Let's look back for a moment.

We've moved from jarred baby food to plastic containers and pouches. From selling it at room temperature to selling it in the refrigerated food section. We've moved from starting baby with pureed foods to beginning the journey with whole foods. We've switched from a slow introduction of new foods to quick transitions that help build food variety from the get-go. We've even changed the stance on what can be eaten in the first year of life, promoting the early introduction of foods previously thought to cause allergy.

Yes, starting baby food and feeding your baby has undergone some significant changes over the last two decades since I was a young mother. We simply have more research behind the topic and know more now than we ever did before.

We have a better sense of nutrients needed for optimal brain development. We have clear ideas about how to prevent picky eating and iron deficiency. We know how to shape flavor preferences and instill healthy eating habits.

In short, we know *exactly* what it takes to get your baby started on the healthiest food and the best, most productive feeding plan for his future health.

Yet, there's a downside to this newfound, changing information for your baby.

It's made starting solids a whole new frontier: daunting, confusing, and sometimes, downright scary.

Scary enough to make you think about holding off on starting your baby on food.

Delay the whole process.

But, delaying has its drawbacks, too. Delaying your baby may stall his developmental milestones, like speaking and fine motor skills and can even set him back, nutritionally.

You don't want to delay.

As the science shifts, you may feel your well-thought-out game plan is on shaky ground, or even, has fallen apart. You may be unsure about starting solids and question whether you have the latest and greatest tools and techniques.

You look to books and the web for all this data. Or you ask your parents for advice, or your friends and colleagues. This is where it starts to get even more confusing....

One mom tells you to avoid baby food altogether, while a popular blogger says make your own and start now. Meanwhile, your doctor says, "wait for the signs," and your well-meaning parent tells you to put cereal in the bottle. You're not quite sure what the "signs" are and you're unsure about putting extra food in your baby's bottle.

You start looking around. You find information on the Internet about arsenic in rice and Baby Led Weaning, but you don't know exactly how to put this information into play with your own baby.

...Meanwhile, the clock is ticking...

All this data – conflicting, confusing and piece-meal-- needs to be pulled together so you have complete information.

Obviously, the more you know about your baby's nutrition, the better job you can do feeding him. You already know this. But, adapting to and adopting this information can be stressful, too. Yes, downright *stressful*.

While major health organizations like the American Academy of Pediatrics (AAP) recommend starting your baby on solid food around 6 months, even this recommendation can feel like a big question mark.

A 2015 survey by Beech-Nut Nutrition Company found that 54% of parents reported being "very confused" with the prospect of starting solids. Parents were especially concerned about the timing of solid food introduction, choosing the right foods to support their baby's future health, getting baby to eat fruits and vegetables, and making sure baby got the right amounts of protein during the transition.

That's where this baby food guide comes in: to set the record straight and clear up any confusion you may have when it comes to starting solids with your baby. And, to help you do it right.

As a pediatric dietitian, I feel it's my job to lay out all the options, considerations, and warnings. It's not my job to tell you to start solids in a certain way. It's not my job to scare you, guilt you, convince you of my perspective, or inform you in ways that could be misleading.

I want you to have all the information you need to do this critical part of infancy and childhood the best way you can for your baby, you, and your family. As such, I have asked for a critical review of this guide by other professionals who work with infants and toddlers in nutrition and in feeding therapy.

In *The Smart Mom's Guide to Starting Solids*, you will learn about your baby's readiness for solids and how her development changes over time, setting the stage for when to begin solids and how to encourage a liking of different flavors. You'll learn the different methods you can use to feed your baby, and the nutrition you need to get clear on before you begin.

You'll learn that *how* you feed your baby sets the foundation for future food preferences and may even prevent picky eating later.

You will learn about the unique and important nutrient needs of your baby and how food can sustain your baby's growth and development. And, you'll get the latest research-based advice for starting solids, advancing them, and making the feeding process a boon for connecting with your baby.

I also give you the latest recommendations on your questions about peanuts, arsenic, fish, transitioning to the cup, the family table, and more.

My goal is to make you a *Smart Mom*. A mom who knows *exactly* how to start solids, progressively advance them, and nourish your baby from the beginning, so you start your baby off on the healthiest foundation you possibly can.

Let's dig in!

Section One

Your Baby: What You Need to Know

Before we dig in to all the details about starting solids, it's important you understand your baby's growth and nutritional requirements. There is a lot going on in the first year of life, but especially during the second half.

In Chapter 1, I focus on helping you understand your baby's growth, development, and the signs he or she is ready to start solids. This is essential for starting on time and meeting your baby's nutritional needs. After that, in Chapter 2, we take a deep dive into nutrition, especially calories, protein and essential nutrients. I've tried to strike a balance of "need to know" information with "how to put it into practice" guidelines in this section. In Chapter 3, I cover what your baby is learning in the process of starting solids. I want you to understand this, as I think it will help you be a more sensitive and understanding parent as you move through the first year of feeding.

Let's begin!

1

Your Baby's Dynamic Growth, Inside and Out

Your baby will grow an amazing amount in his first year of life. When you look at the statistics, it's staggering. Yes, staggering. Your baby will triple his birth weight. His length will increase by 55% and his head circumference (the measurement around the crown of the head) will grow 40% more by the end of the year. There is an enormous amount of growth that occurs by your baby's first birthday! After this first year, growth slows down to about half the rate of the first year.

Organs grow, too, and their ability to function matures, allowing more complex food to be processed and used by the body. Developmentally, your baby will become more aware, learn how to chew more complex foods, and feed himself. There are a lot of changes happening in this magical first year!

The most important thing to remember: there's a steep learning curve for both you and your baby. You will learn about your baby—what he likes, how he relates to food, and how to connect with him. Your baby will learn about flavor, textures, and whether you are a reliable source of sustenance. He will also learn about eating and associate pleasure or negative thoughts with the experience.

Your Baby is Growing, Fast

Baby's growth takes center-stage during the first year, making calories and nutrients important considerations as you begin your feeding journey. If your baby is able to nurse, the recommendations are to continue with breastfeeding through the first year of life. Breastfeed for as long as you are willing and able. Your baby will be getting his calories and nutrients from your breast milk during the time you are exclusively breast feeding. The same is true for formula-fed babies in the liquid nutrition phase.

Your baby's nutrient needs, however, climb to a higher level beginning around 6 months, which is why "complementary" foods, or solid foods, are introduced—they give the additional nutrients your baby needs.

You might wonder if breast milk is still good. Yes, it's still a great way to nourish your baby. However, you'll need to offer solids or another source of nutrients to match your baby's higher nutritional requirements. Nursing and starting solids at 6 months *complement* each other.

Remember, breastfeeding is a wonderful way to connect with your baby. It also offers unique immunological properties and a natural way to develop responsive feeding. However, connection and meaningful feeding can happen whether you are breastfeeding or formula feeding...it's all about being responsive! We'll discuss responsive feeding later in this guide.

As your baby eats more solid food, her reliance on breast milk or formula will gradually decrease. This is normal and often happens without much intervention from you.

Changes Happen on the Inside

Between 4 and 6 months of age, physical changes occur in your baby's body allowing the introduction of solid food. Once you understand that your baby is physiologically ready to start solids, some of your fear will melt away.

Here's what you can expect around 6 months of age:

1. Your baby's intestinal tract matures and can protect him against infections and allergies to the proteins in food. It's also able to process food better. Digestion and absorption of nutrients such as protein, fat and carbohydrate increases rapidly.

2. Your baby's kidneys are better able to handle meats, which have a high renal solute load (renal solutes are nutrients that are processed through the kidney). It is not recommended to offer meats before 6 months of age. If an infant's kidneys are not mature enough it places her at risk for dehydration.

3. Your baby gains more control of his neuromuscular system, which allows him to eat off a spoon, chew, and swallow solid foods. He also begins to recognize food and associate flavors and textures with pleasure (or not).

Developmental Changes Indicate Readiness

Professionals like myself gauge a baby's readiness to start solids by looking at where the baby is on the developmental spectrum.

These developmental indicators signal your baby is ready to begin eating solid food. They indicate your baby can take on more texture, and begin to mash and chew food.

Your baby:

✓ Is able to sit up, by himself, or with support

✓ Is able to open his mouth when he sees food coming

✓ Is able to position his tongue (low and flat) to receive food

✓ Is able to close his lips around food on a spoon and scrape food off the spoon as it is removed from the mouth

- ✓ Is able to keep food in his mouth, rather than spit it out. The tongue thrust reflex disappears around age 4 to 6 months, allowing food to be moved to the back of the mouth for swallowing

- ✓ The gag reflex relaxes and is settled at the back third of the tongue

- ✓ The tongue moves to the left and right side of the mouth (rather than forward and back) and a chewing motion starts to emerge

- ✓ Baby's tongue can move up, down and side to side in response to something in his mouth

- ✓ The tongue can move items to the sides of the mouth to promote chewing

- ✓ Your baby's front teeth (top and bottom), and the side teeth may be erupting

- ✓ The jaw begins to move in a diagonal rotary direction

Most importantly, every baby is different. Just because your baby is a certain age, doesn't necessarily mean he's ready to start solids. And, if your baby is showing *all* the signs of readiness early, it doesn't mean you need to hold him off.

Some babies take a little bit longer to be ready, and others are ready earlier. However, babies are *not ready* to eat solids before 4 months, so sit tight and let your baby mature a bit more.

Additionally, some babies may start later, based on other situations such as prematurity, low birth weight, frequent hospitalizations, poor growth (also called Failure to Thrive), neuromuscular delays, abuse or neglect, or an inability to eat by mouth due to a medical condition. If this is the case with your baby, rest assured he will eventually get there-- it just may take a little more time.

2

Your Baby's Nutritional Needs

Before we get into baby food and the introduction of it, you also need to understand your baby's nutritional requirements. That is, his calorie and nutrient needs. All babies, regardless of the chosen method of feeding, need adequate calories and protein to grow, and they have certain critical nutrients that need to be met in the first year of life.

Calories and Protein

You'll enjoy hearing this news: calories and protein sort themselves out, for the most part.

If you let your baby lead with his appetite, he'll most likely let you know when he's hungry and when he's had enough to eat. This internal appetite barometer is hard-wired from the get-go, and you need not do much to adjust it, other than carefully listen, understand, and be aware of your baby's appetite cues.

I'll cover your baby's appetite signals in a bit.

Calories and protein are included in sufficient amounts in breast milk and formula, provided your baby consumes enough volume. As mentioned above, during the early transitional months of starting solids, your baby will still get most of his calories from liquid sources of nutrition. As he starts to eat more solids, the contribution of calories and protein from breast milk or formula will naturally decrease, while the calories from solids foods increase and balance themselves.

Your breastfed baby is getting enough breast milk if:

- ✓ He is gaining weight

- ✓ As a newborn, he is nursing at least 8 times in 24 hours

- ✓ He is nursing every 2 to 3 hours, for 10-15 minutes on each breast

- ✓ He has several wet diapers each day (and several bowel movements)

- ✓ He seems satisfied after nursing

Your formula fed baby is getting enough if:

- ✓ He is gaining weight

- ✓ He is drinking a bottle every 2 to 3 hours

- ✓ He has several wet diapers each day (and a few bowel movements)

- ✓ He seems satisfied after eating

- ✓ He is consuming at least 2 ½ to 3 ounces of formula per pound each day (8# baby would consume at least 20 to 24 ounces per day)

While your baby still gets the lion share of nutrition from breast milk or formula, solid foods will close the gap on those nutrients from breastmilk that start to fall short of your baby's needs.

During the initial stages of starting solids, the goal is to let your baby have the experience of different textures and flavors, while learning the coordinated skills involved in eating. Amazingly, your baby will learn these quickly and the amounts of food he ingests will steadily increase (and he'll rely less on liquid nutrition as his sole source of nutrients).

Note: As your baby grows and his weight increases, the amount of formula he consumes will increase, up to 32 ounces per day. At this point, your baby may be ready to start solid food.

Important Nutrients

In addition to calories and protein, certain nutrients are important to consider when starting solids and meeting your baby's nutritional needs. These nutrients stand out because they are critical in the first year of development, especially for the brain and bones.

Read on for a quick tutorial!

Iron is for Intelligence

Iron requirements are particularly important during the first year of life when baby's brain is developing, his body is growing, and iron stores are being built up.

At birth, your baby is theoretically "loaded" with sufficient iron to get her through the first 6 to 8 months of life. This depends, however, on a few things: your own iron stores and iron status during pregnancy, whether your baby was born prematurely, and the timing of the umbilical cord clamping.

Early clamping reduces blood volume delivery to baby while *delayed clamping* (2-3 minutes after birth) allows your baby to receive about 30-50% of total blood volume from the placenta. In plain English, delayed clamping allows your baby to get a bigger iron dose from you at birth.

From the fourth month on, your baby's iron stores are used up rapidly because she is experiencing tremendous physical growth, and as such, expanding her blood volume quickly, while developing her own iron stores. This is the reason the AAP recommends beginning breastfed babies on an iron supplement at age four months.

In humans, iron is preferentially reserved for the blood, at the expense of the brain's requirements for cognitive development. Experts note that iron deficiency may be difficult to assess in infancy due to rapid changes in body composition. However, the data on iron deficiency is telling. Fourteen percent of children under the age of two years are iron deficient in the United States. Twelve percent of babies aged 6 to 11 months have inadequate intakes as compared to the Recommended Daily Allowance (RDA).

In children under age 4 who live in industrialized countries (hello, USA), it's estimated that about 20% are iron deficient. More than 9% of the entire US population is iron deficient.

There are two sources of iron from food: heme and non-heme iron. Heme iron comes from animal sources, and are naturally well-absorbed in the body. Non-heme iron comes from plant foods and need some help for optimal absorption. Vitamin C food sources like citrus fruits are the ideal helpers in this scenario.

Good sources of heme iron are: oysters, beef cuts and ground beef, turkey (dark meat), tuna canned in water, turkey (light meat), chicken (light and dark meat), fresh tuna, crab, pork, shrimp, and halibut.

Good sources of non-heme iron: ready-to-eat cereals, oatmeal, soybeans, lentils, beans (kidney, lima, black-eyed peas, navy, black, pinto), tofu, spinach, raisins, molasses, and commercially prepared white and wheat bread.

Vitamin C comes from a variety of foods including tomatoes and tomato products, citrus fruits and juices, and other fruits and vegetables. See Appendix for a listing of vitamin C foods.

Iron Needs Change Mid-Year

Around 6 months of age, iron requirements increase significantly to 11 mg/day (from 0.27 mg/day), making iron an important consideration when choosing the first foods to feed your baby.

If you are breastfeeding, iron-rich foods will play a central role to your baby's overall growth and development. You'll want to try to offer two servings of iron-containing foods each day.

If you are offering plant-based iron sources (non-heme foods), give a source of vitamin C (orange juice, peaches, or tomato sauce, etc) at the same time to maximize iron absorption.

Some parents alleviate their concerns about iron, vitamin C and other nutrients by giving their child a liquid multivitamin that contains these and other important nutrients. A word of caution: Make sure you're not overloading your baby with nutrients. Certain nutrients, like vitamin A can be toxic to your baby when received in high doses from food, supplements, or a combination of both.

If your baby is bottle-fed, be sure to choose an infant formula that is fortified with iron. This will generally provide adequate amounts of iron. Even though, you will still want to introduce quality iron-containing food sources during the 6 to 12 month stage and after.

Iron Needs During the First Year

Age	Iron Requirements	Food Sources
0-6 mo. 6-12 mo.	0.27 mg/day 11 mg/day	Heme: oysters, beef cuts and ground beef, turkey (dark meat), tuna canned in water, turkey (light meat), chicken (light and dark meat), fresh tuna, crab, pork, shrimp, and halibut Non-heme: ready-to-eat cereals, iron-fortified baby cereal; oatmeal, soybeans, lentils, beans (kidney, lima, black-eyed peas, navy, black, pinto), tofu, spinach, blackstrap molasses, and commercially prepared white and wheat bread; Iron-fortified infant formula

What Happens When Iron Needs Are Not Met?

The breastfed baby may be at higher risk for iron deficiency and iron deficiency anemia, especially if complementary food sources of iron are not included routinely in the diet or an external source is not routinely provided. Unfortunately, some babies don't get enough iron in their diet until later in the first year, which may have negative consequences.

Research suggests when young children are iron-deficient or have iron deficiency anemia, their health may suffer, including changes in their immune status, delayed mental development, and below average school achievements.

As I mentioned, this happens partly because there is a preferential use of iron in the body to make hemoglobin (a protein found in red blood cells which carries oxygen to cells and organs in the body). Making hemoglobin is a priority and may lead to a redirection of iron away from the brain, particularly when iron intake is low in the diet.

The American Academy of Pediatrics (AAP) now screens for iron-deficiency anemia at 12 months, stating,

"There is growing evidence that iron deficiency and iron deficiency anemia have long-term effects on behavioral and neurodevelopmental issues that can appear one to two decades after the anemia is treated."

Complementary foods, otherwise known as solids, should begin at 6 months to help assure babies receive adequate iron. Babies who are breastfed should begin an iron supplement at 4 months of age (1 milligram per kilogram body weight) to ensure adequate iron is received, in addition to beginning iron-rich first foods.

Zinc is for Growth and Immunity

Zinc is a key nutrient for growth and appetite. Young children with poor zinc intake may grow slowly and have a poor appetite causing inadequate food intake. Zinc is also tied to immunity and plays a role in keeping your baby healthy.

Infants aged 0-6 months need 2 mg of zinc each day and those aged 6-12 months need to get 3 mg zinc each day, according to the Institute of Medicine (IOM) Dietary Reference Intakes (DRI).

If you are breastfeeding, your breast milk contains enough zinc to nourish your baby during his first 6 months of life. The zinc in breast milk is well absorbed and utilized, or highly bioavailable.

At 6 months, however, the zinc supplied by breast milk decreases somewhat, while your baby's requirements increase, much like the situation with iron. Introducing solid foods around 6 months will help ensure your baby continues to receive enough zinc for his growth and development. Six percent of older babies do not meet the Estimated Average Requirement (EAR) for zinc.

All babies who begin solid foods should be introduced to zinc-rich foods. Foods like red meat, zinc-fortified baby cereal, certain cooked seafood, and mashed beans are good sources of zinc to offer when beginning solids. Families who choose to use organic cereals may note that many are not fortified with zinc.

By age 9 months, your baby should be getting most (90%) of his iron and zinc requirements from food sources, so be sure to focus on the foods that can supply both.

If your baby is bottle-feeding, infant formula will contain adequate amounts of zinc if your baby is consuming recommended amounts.

Zinc Needs During the First Year

Age	Zinc Needs	Food Sources
0-6 months	2 mg/day	Beef, lamb, chicken, turkey, crabmeat, lobster, fortified ready-to-eat breakfast cereals, beans, nuts, whole grains and foods made with whole grains, dairy products; infant formula
6-12 months	3 mg/day	

Fat is for Growth and Brain Development

Your baby needs quite a bit of fat in her diet to sustain her rapid growth in the first year of life, especially when considering how small her tummy is and how quickly it fills up! Every calorie counts and fat is a concentrated source of calories.

In fact, babies need about 50% of their total calories from fat, which is an amount naturally found in breast milk and infant formula. However, when babies start solid food, their fluid intake naturally decreases over time, making fat sources from solid food an important inclusion.

Fat is a satiating nutrient so it helps your baby feel full and satisfied after eating. It also helps your baby absorb the fat-soluble vitamins A, D, E and K.

Fat Needs During the First Year of Life

Age	Fat Needs	Food Sources
0-6 months	31 grams/day*	Breast milk, infant formula, butter, margarine, olive oil, plant oils, full-fat yogurt, cheese, whole milk, visible fat on meats and poultry, nut butters, avocado, plant oils
7-12 months	30 grams/day*	

*Adequate Intake

Dietary Reference Intakes for Energy, Carbohydrate. Fiber, Fat, Fatty Acids, Cholesterol, Protein, and Amino Acids (2002/2005)

A Special Kind of Fat

Docosahexaenoic acid (DHA) is an omega-3 polyunsaturated fatty acid (a type of fat) found in the brain. It influences brain functioning in many ways, such as sending messages throughout the brain (called neurotransmission) and growing new connections and pathways for those messages (called neurogenesis).

DHA is also a critical nutrient in the development of your baby's vision, especially since it acts as a structural component to the retina of the eye.

Let's focus on the brain, though.

The brain is lipid rich—in other words, it's full of fat. Research suggests more than half of the brain is made up of fat, especially the long-chain omega-3 polyunsaturated fatty acids (PUFAs). Of those PUFAs in the brain, DHA is the most significant fatty acid.

Babies are born with stores of DHA in the brain, which accumulate in pregnancy. During early infancy, rapid accumulation of DHA in the brain persists. Researchers believe that optimal levels of DHA, particularly in the frontal and prefrontal areas of the brain, are very important during the early years when the brain is rapidly growing and developing, and hence, setting the stage for future intelligence and socio-emotional development. However, the research on this aspect is inconclusive at this time.

When I say future intelligence, I'm referring to your child's cognition. The word cognition encompasses a wide variety of brain abilities. For example, it includes your child's ability to pay attention, remember what he's learned, and his language development.

Cognition also includes problem solving, comprehension, reasoning, computation, perception, reading and speech.

As you can see, setting the stage for cognitive development in the first year of life may directly impact your child's future intellectual abilities, thinking and performance, future success in school --and all areas of his or her life.

One way you can do this is to breast feed your baby for the first year. However, *you* need to be focused on getting adequate DHA in your diet as well, as this directly influences the quality and quantity of DHA your baby receives.

I've included the DHA requirements for pregnant and breastfeeding moms in the chart below. If breastfeeding is not in the plan, then choose an infant formula that is fortified with DHA.

Unfortunately, surveys suggest the diets of children in the United States are lacking in DHA. According to the 2015 Dietary Guidelines for Americans (DGA), most infants and young toddlers aged 1-3 years are *not* meeting the recommended intake levels of DHA.

It's important to include DHA routinely in the diet, especially as you branch out to solid foods!

DHA Needs for Mom and Tot

Pregnant & Breastfeeding Moms	200 mg DHA per day 8-12 oz. seafood per week*
Babies, 0-6 months	0.1-0.18% of total energy intake
Babies, 6-24 months	10 - 12 mg/kg/day of DHA, or 4.5 – 5.5 mg/pound/day

*USDA recommendations

Be sure to include fat sources in your baby's daily meal plan by including plant oils, avocado, nut butter, butter, whole milk (wait until a year old) and yogurt.

To maximize on DHA consumption, include fatty fish (especially salmon, mackerel, sardines, and herring), fish oil, meat and DHA-fortified eggs.

For your baby or toddler (6 months to 2 years), 3 - 4 ounces of seafood per week will help you achieve an adequate DHA intake.

If that's not in the cards, consider a supplement that either includes DHA singularly or a fish oil supplement that provides a combination of EPA (eicosapentaenoic acid) and DHA.

Vitamin D is for Bones and More

Studies suggest 10 to 78% of babies who do not receive a vitamin D supplement within the first few days of life are deficient in this nutrient. Unfortunately, in my practice, I see plenty of babies who are not getting supplemental vitamin D.

Rickets is making a comeback, slowly but surely. Rickets is a softening of the bones in the legs causing a bow-legged appearance and is caused by a deficiency of vitamin D.

At birth, your baby's bones are soft. Calcium helps them harden, but vitamin D is needed to make sure calcium is carried into the bone.

The latest prevalence statistics of Rickets is 24 per 100,000, which doesn't sound like a lot, but this is increased over recent decades, and is totally preventable. Rickets is associated with race (it is more common in African Americans), breastfeeding, low birth weight, and stunted growth/short stature. Vitamin D deficiency is also associated with poor immunity, poor bone health, and chronic disease.

All babies who are breastfed or partially breastfed (using both breast-milk and infant formula) should be receiving a vitamin D supplement in the amount of 400 IU per day, started right after birth, and continuing until your baby is consuming about 32 ounces of vitamin D fortified milk or infant formula daily.

If your baby is consuming infant formula, vitamin D is included as part of the panel of nutrients, but extra may be prudent until your baby is consuming a liter of formula daily.

Vitamin D Needs in the First Year

Age	Vitamin D Requirements	Food Sources
0-6 months	400 IU	Salmon, cooked mushrooms, eggs, vitamin D-fortified milk or orange juice; infant formula
6-12 months	400 IU	

Vitamin D requirements are very hard to meet with food sources alone. One reason is that there are not many natural sources of vitamin D. Thankfully, we have several fortified foods such as milk, some yogurts, ready-to-eat cereal, and more.

Sunshine activates vitamin D in the skin, which is a natural way to accrue vitamin D. However, the recommended use of sunscreen for infants means babies can't rely on sunshine as a source of vitamin D.

As your baby transitions to solids, keep an eye out for foods that include vitamin D, either naturally (fatty fish such as salmon, cooked mushrooms, or eggs) or from fortified foods (milk, or vitamin D-fortified orange juice).

As you reach the one year milestone, milk or milk alternatives fortified with vitamin D will help your baby match his requirements, though you may still need supplementation to assure he's getting enough.

If you are worried your baby may have a low vitamin D level, ask your doctor about checking it. Vitamin D deficiency is very hard to detect, as it doesn't cause obvious symptoms unless it has progressed. If vitamin D levels are low, a supplement will be needed to normalize levels quickly, as food sources don't do a good job of replenishing these levels (this goes for iron deficiency, too).

Calcium is for Bones

Calcium is an essential nutrient for bone development, among other critical functions in the body. If you are breastfeeding your baby, it's important that *your* diet is adequate in calcium, as you are your baby's source of calcium. If you don't consume enough calcium in your diet, your body will pull calcium from your bones to make it available for your breast milk and your baby. This process places you at risk for poor bone density later.

If you are using infant formula, your baby's calcium needs will be met if he or she consumes adequate amounts for her age.

Calcium Needs in the First Year

Age	Calcium Requirements	Food Sources
0-6 months	200 mg/day (AI)	Milk, yogurt, cheese, spinach, broccoli; infant formula
6-12 months	260 mg/day (AI)	

*Adequate Intake (AI): the established amount to meet requirements; there is no RDA/DRI for calcium in infants.

Fortunately, intake data tells us that calcium requirements are generally met in the first two years of life. This is probably due to the higher milk, yogurt and cheese consumption at this stage.

Keep up the good work if you're matching your baby's calcium needs! But, beware that after age two, calcium intake drops in most children and by childhood it becomes an "at risk nutrient," unfortunately staying that way through adulthood.

Including regular sources of calcium in your baby's diet and continuing to do so throughout childhood will moderate the risks of low calcium intake down the road.

Fiber is for Regularity

Currently, there are no recommendations for fiber intake for infants in the first year of life. In fact, your baby's digestive system is developing and still maturing and not ready for hefty doses of fiber in the first 4 to 6 months.

At 6 months of age, when you initiate solid food introduction, your baby will receive small amounts of fiber from fortified cereals, pureed fruit and vegetables. As you advance through increasing texture and food variety in the second half of the year (7-12 months), fiber will naturally make its way into your baby's diet. For example, at around 10 months, your baby can eat diced ripe banana, ripe pears, cooked carrots and squash, all of which are good sources of fiber.

A Plant-Based Approach

The AAP and the Academy of Nutrition and Dietetics (AND) both agree that plant-based diets when "appropriately planned...are healthful, nutritionally adequate and may provide health benefits... during all stages of the life cycle."

If you are planning to raise your baby using a plant-based diet, make sure to pay attention to these nutrients: vitamin B_{12}, vitamin D, calcium, iron, fluoride, DHA and overall protein.

Your baby can get vitamin B_{12} from milk, eggs, soymilk, cereal, meat substitutes or a supplement. Offer fluoridated water or a fluoride supplement for breastfed babies who drink little water. The remaining food sources of vitamin D, calcium, iron, DHA and protein are mentioned later in this book.

Take-Aways:

Your baby grows rapidly in the first year, unlike any other time in childhood (except adolescence), making calories and nutrients critical considerations of feeding.

Many key nutrients, such as iron, zinc, calcium, vitamin D and DHA are critical to your baby's growth and cognitive development.

3

Your Baby is Learning to Eat

Babies and young toddlers have a fast learning curve when it comes to eating solid food. After 6 months of age, eating is a learned endeavor and it takes the coordination of eight sensory systems.

When you think about it, from ages 6 months to one year—a 6-month time span—your baby will move from pureed food to table food. He will also learn to feed himself and drink from a cup. That's a lot of food learning in 6 months!

Food Helps Your Baby Learn to Chew

In the first 6 months of life, your baby's mouth muscles have mastered sucking. To learn how to chew and talk, those muscles must be challenged. Moving from pureed food to whole, chopped foods teaches your baby how to chew and swallow solids.

Additionally, the texture of food reinforces these newfound skills of mashing and chewing, helping your baby exercise his mouth muscles and lay the groundwork for speech and language.

It's important to introduce more food texture, including chunkier foods and chopped foods in the second half of year one. When babies don't receive table foods between 8 and 12 months, they may experience more difficulty with eating later. One study showed that if lumpy foods weren't introduced by 9 months of age, problems with feeding were more likely at age seven.

When the mouth muscles aren't challenged with chewing, mashing and moving food around in the mouth, the risk for a speech delay or a feeding problem increases. Learning how to chew is a precursor for language development and eating mastery. But, don't start pushing your baby to chew earlier than he is ready!

At around 8-9 months, most babies will have the ability to advance along with more challenging food textures. If your baby is not eating pureed foods by 10 months and/or not eating table foods by one year, you may need to assess his development and explore feeding therapy.

A word on baby food pouches

Parents love them. They are convenient, flavorful, an easy way to check off the fruit and veggie category and in many cases, are less messy. However, many healthcare professionals cringe over them. Why? Because baby food or puree pouches have the potential to be abused, relied (too heavily) on, may cause choking, and can stall your baby's development.

Think about it: a baby food pouch has one texture and offers one dimension of feeding. Pouch food is pureed for the most part (some offering a bit more texture with chia or other grains added) and prevents interaction with food, relying on a sucking mechanism for consumption.

If you've discovered the magic of baby food pouches, keep a few tips in mind:

- ✓ Use them infrequently-- in a pinch, or for travel

- ✓ Feed them to your baby on a spoon (that is/was the intention behind this product!)

- ✓ Mix them with other textured food, such as a veggie pouch mixed with mashed beans or chopped meat

✓ Sit down without distractions when eating them

✓ Be with your baby if he is eating them independently due to the risk of choking

Learning About Your Baby's Appetite

Trying to read your baby's cues can be confusing. He cries and wiggles and fusses. What does that mean? Is he wet? Bored? Or hungry? Mastering the appetite cues of hunger and fullness will help you be more tuned in, responsive and in sync with feeding your baby.

How do I know if my baby is hungry?

Your baby fusses or cries.

Fussy, crying babies are often regarded as hungry. Be careful though-- fussing or crying doesn't always equal hunger. It can mean other things such as discomfort, tiredness or even boredom.

Your baby smiles, gazes or coos at you during a feeding.

This is a sign your baby is enjoying her food and wants to continue eating.

Your baby moves her head toward the spoon or bottle.

This is a pretty clear indication that your baby wants to eat and is hungry.

Your baby reaches for or points to food.

As your baby gets a bit older, she will be clearer about her desire to eat. While pointing may not mean hunger (she might like a food and want to eat it, even though she just ate), it gives you the indication that she is learning to connect food with appetite and eating.

Your baby shows excitement when food is offered.

Again, your baby is responding to food and this may be a sign she is ready to eat.

Your baby uses sounds, words, or signs to indicate hunger.

At the end of infancy, it gets easier to read your baby's hunger cues, as she can communicate in multiple ways.

How do I know if my baby is full?

Your baby decreases the rate of sucking or stops sucking.

Slowing the rate of eating is a sign that fullness is closing in. Try not to force the rest of the bottle, as this may overfeed her.

Your baby spits out the nipple.

This is a clear sign of being full and done with eating.

Your baby becomes easily distracted or pays more attention to the environment around her.

In general, young children eat vigorously when they are hungry and consume a great percentage of the calories early in the meal. It's important to minimize distractions at feeding sessions so that you can read your baby's appetite and your baby can focus on eating.

Your baby moves her head away from food.

When your baby is older and eating solid foods, dodging the spoon or slouching away from food may be a sign of fullness.

Your baby slows the pace of eating.

As with liquid feedings, when your baby is eating solids and is approaching fullness, she will slow down the rate of her food consumption.

Fortunately, as your baby gets older, it becomes easier to recognize her fullness. For example, she may bat at the spoon, turn her head away, clench her mouth shut, shake her head to say no, play with food, throw it, or just simply say "no" or "all done."

These signs indicate your baby has reached her stopping point. If it worries you that she hasn't eaten enough, remember that your baby eats frequently throughout the day and she has many opportunities to accumulate her nutritional needs and make up any deficits along the way. We'll cover the structure and frequency of meals and snacks later in this book.

Flavor Builds Your Baby's Food Preferences

In the first six months of life, if your baby is breast fed, he will experience the flavors of your diet, and this may transition to greater food acceptance when he starts to eat real food. If he is formula-fed, his exposure to different flavors is limited by the fact that formula flavor doesn't change.

Research shows that exposure to a variety of different flavors helps lay the foundation for what your baby will be willing to eat later. In fact, researchers have identified a "flavor window" – the timing when babies are most sensitive and receptive to incorporating different flavors into their diet. This flavor window is between 4 and 18 months.

When your baby starts to eat solids, regardless of whether he was breastfed or formula fed, introducing a variety of different flavors through feeding in the first year is the name of the game. Further research indicates that when babies eat blended baby food (carrots + apricots, e.g.), they are more food adventurous than babies who eat single flavor baby food (carrots).

Introduce as much variety within food groups as possible. Why? Your baby will get more nutrients, quickly get used to different flavors, and possibly be less picky later. This honeymoon phase of eating, when your baby likes almost everything you offer, won't last forever, so make it work for you and her!

In addition to that, as your baby advances through more complex food, you'll want to spice it up. Do not be shy in the spicy, savory, umami flavor categories. Research tells us that the more flavor and aromatics your baby tastes, the better acceptance he or she will have to new food down the road.

To help you take flavor variety up a notch, I've included a herb, spice and food pairing chart by Clancy Harrison, author and creator of the online course *Feed Your Baby, Save Your Sanity*, in the Appendix of this book.

Preserving Your Baby's Self-Regulation

As I mentioned earlier, your baby is born with an internal appetite regulator—in other words, he knows when to eat, how much to eat, and when to stop eating.

Researchers call this self-regulation.

A self-regulated eater means that your baby can control his own eating by being tuned into and supported in his appetite. Being good at self-regulation is a key to healthy eating and a healthy weight down the road. It relies on your ability to be responsive with feeding and your understanding of your baby's appetite.

It's important to preserve this natural sense of appetite intuition because it translates to the eating habits of your child when he is older. Feeding your baby, whether by spoon or with self-feeding approaches, as I'll explain later, can be supportive to this end-goal.

Your feeding approach may also change your baby's appetite regulation, especially if you are keen on getting your baby to finish his bottle or eat all his food. Pushing your baby to drain the bottle or finish the baby food container can teach him to overeat. This is another topic we will cover later in this book.

Be sure to pay attention to your baby's signs of hunger and fullness, and respond to them appropriately. That is the key to supporting his self-regulation.

Your Baby Learns to Self-Feed

Starting solids is made easier by the development of the palmer and pincer grasps. The palmer grasp is your baby's ability to push food or another object into his palm using his fingers. This develops around 6 months of age.

Between 6 and 8 months, the pincer grasp emerges. This is the ability to hold an object between the thumb and forefinger. Once this develops, it's an indication your baby is ready to advance to some diced or chopped foods. When these fine motor skills emerge, you'll see your baby's ability to self-feed take off!

Need some inspiration for ideal foods for self-feeding?

Try cubes of banana; chopped, cooked pasta; strings of cheese; smashed beans or blueberries.

If spoon-feeding has been the norm for quite a while (beyond 8 months), and your baby relies on you to deliver food to him, he may be slow to feed himself, or even refuse to be independent in this area. Watch for the signs of readiness, and try to move forward with food as soon as your baby shows developmental milestones and skills. Don't be afraid to challenge your baby and allow her to have some time to work on her self-feeding skills.

Take-Aways:

Your baby is learning quite a bit about food, his appetite, and eating in the second half of the first year.

Building food preferences for a variety of food happens in the first year of life and beyond, into preschool. Your child is particularly receptive to a variety of flavors between 4 and 18 months. A child's food preferences are largely set by age five.

Your child has an innate ability to self-regulate his food consumption. Your job is to support and sustain this by staying responsive in feeding.

Section Two

Getting Ready to Start Solids

Let's be honest, the questions are circling in your head. You may even lay awake at night thinking about starting solids.

Is it time to begin? Is my baby ready? I think so, but I'm not sure.

The goal of this section is to calm your worries and help you get clear on the timing of that first bite! I also spend time on the mistakes that can happen during this early stage so you can avoid them. This section builds on the last, setting the stage with information that will help you be smart, sensitive and informed.

In Chapter 4, I cover the signs of readiness, from age standards to the developmental cues that tell you, *Yes, it's time.* Chapter 5 takes your nutrition knowledge to a higher level by simplifying food to showcase nutrient partners so you can begin to strategize smart food choices for your baby. Chapter 6 gives you lowdown on feeding—how to be responsive, your feeding style, your everyday feeding practices, and the mistakes to avoid.

4

Is It Time to Begin?

You've been nursing or bottle-feeding for a while now, and we can assume you and your baby have hit your stride. You're both comfortable, things have a rhythm, and honestly, everything is predictable. Cut and dry. You even have a predictable time when you can grab a shower!

You're starting to sense change is on the horizon. You are thinking about starting solids.

Start with Age

Major health organizations like the American Academy of Pediatrics (AAP) recommend waiting to introduce solids until about 6 months of age. This is a solid recommendation for most infants.

However, some babies will show all the signs of readiness for solids earlier. My own son did, which drove me to hunt for more answers. I certainly didn't want to go against recommendations.

Readiness for Solids Matters Most

As you read earlier, the digestive tract is ready for solid food around 4 to 6 months, and developmental readiness (oral motor, gross motor and fine motor skills) can appear between 4 and 6 months, as well. Readiness for solids may appear in these two categories at the same time, which is why experts say your baby may start solids between 4 and 6 months.

The body of research suggests it is safe to introduce solids anywhere from 4 to 6 months depending on the signals your baby is showing you.

In *Fearless Feeding*, my co-author and I recommend five to six months as a reasonable time to start solids, particularly if the signs of readiness are apparent.

You can see, the best time to start solids is less about a hard and fast age, but more about your baby's developmental readiness. If you need a reminder of the general signs of readiness, refer to Chapter xx.

Take-Away:

Start solids around 6 months.

If you start before 6 months, make sure your baby is showing the signs of readiness outlined earlier. Some babies who start early when not ready have a negative experience with eating, which can deter enjoyment and progression to table food.

Your baby should *not* start solids before 4 months.

Common Mistakes to Avoid

Starting Solids Too Soon

Some parents believe starting solids will help their baby sleep better at night, so they add cereal to the bottle or initiate mealtime. In fact, up to 40% of parents start feeding solids before 4 months, according to a national survey conducted by the Centers for Disease Control and Prevention (CDC).

Starting your baby on solid food before 4 months introduces food when your baby's immune and digestive systems aren't fully mature or equipped to process food and defend against potential allergens, respectively. As a result, the risk for food allergy, eczema, celiac disease, gastrointestinal infection, and excessive weight gain are higher.

Waiting Too Long to Start Solids

Fear of choking or an allergic reaction to food is enough to give any parent pause. But delaying solids isn't best for baby. As I hinted to earlier, according to a 2009 study in *Maternal & Child Nutrition*, children who didn't advance food texture to a lumpy consistency by 9 months of age had more feeding problems at age 7 than those kids who experienced lumpy textures between ages 6 and 9 months.

Additionally, waiting too long to start solids may slow your baby's growth, increase the risk for iron deficiency, delay eating skills and development, contribute to food texture sensitivities, and may contribute to food allergy development.

Getting Stuck on Purees

Using pureed foods for too long, or spoon-feeding your baby beyond the recommended time frame, has its drawbacks, too. Eating smooth pureed food misses out on the texture variations associated with solid food. Think about rice, pasta, meat or cheese—each of these have varied textures which make baby use his mouth muscles to chew, mash, and maneuver food to the back of his mouth. These actions are integral to the development of muscle strength for more complicated textures and speech.

If you are using commercially-made pureed foods, they may not contain enough calories, especially as your little one downgrades his consumption of breast milk or formula consumption and begins to rely more on solid food for his nutrition.

Take-Away:

Timing is everything! Follow your child's lead and begin solid foods when he or she shows you the signs of readiness.

5

Let Nutrients Guide Your Food Choice

As I discussed earlier, critical nutrients for growth and development need attention, especially when embarking on starting solids. By now, you have a good handle on the important nutrients to pay attention to for your baby. Fortunately, some nutrients go hand-in-hand, which makes it easier to cover and track them when choosing foods for your baby's meals. Consider these "nutrient partners."

As a rule, I encourage all families to let nutrients be one of the first criteria for choosing first foods. If you need a review of each nutrient and its role in your baby's health, see Chapter Two

Iron and Zinc

As I discussed earlier, iron is an essential nutrient in the first year of life. Iron is critical to the growth and development of your baby's brain. Deficiencies in iron can cause irreversible effects on your baby's intellectual potential. I think we've lost sight of this nutrient and its importance in the early years of feeding. Zinc is also important for growth, immunity and appetite.

One of the only foods that provide a source of both iron and zinc is meat, such as beef, dark meat chicken, and turkey. As such, the AAP (and I) recommend it as a first food.

Beans also offer a source of both iron and zinc, however, beans are more difficult for a new eater to digest, and the nutrients are less bioavailable (e.g. they are less efficiently absorbed and utilized by the body). Make sure your baby has some experience with solid foods before introducing beans.

Traditionally, starting baby on rice cereal has been the norm. Iron-fortified cereals are replete with a good source of iron, are easy to digest, proven to defend against iron deficiency, and considered to be low in allergens. Over the years, though, rice cereal has come under scrutiny for its arsenic content and status as a refined grain.

As a result, some parents have rejected it.

However, iron-fortified rice cereal has been studied and found to be a reliant way to ensure baby gets enough iron in the second half of the first year, and a food known to reliably prevent iron-deficiency in infants.

To mitigate the exposure to arsenic from rice cereal, experts suggest rotating different iron-fortified grain-based cereals. For example, use oats, barley, and mixed grains in a rotation with rice cereal. This reduces the exposure to arsenic, overall.

Additionally, some baby cereals also contain zinc, making this a convenient option for providing iron and zinc together.

If you are using a self-feeding approach with your baby, something I'll discuss later, you may want to consider using beef as a first food to help meet adequate sources of iron and zinc.

Bottom line: Offer first foods with a good source of iron and zinc, such as pureed beef or other meat, or iron and zinc-fortified cereal.

Feed your baby two servings of iron-rich foods per day during his transition to solids, regardless of which method of feeding you use, as it will provide a good source of iron.

For example:

4 tablespoons of iron-fortified oatmeal with a cooked egg yolk (7 mg iron), and meat puree with green beans (3 mg).

Fat and DHA

As I discussed, fat is a needed nutrient in the first year, mainly because it's a concentrated calorie source and a nutrient needed by the brain for its optimal development. Depending on the type of fat you choose, it may also be a source of the omega-3 fatty acid DHA, which is tied to intellectual development.

Once you start solids, you'll want to pay attention to including food sources of fat and DHA in your baby's diet.

Food Sources of Fat	Food Sources of DHA
Avocado, chopped olives, olive oil, plant oils, nut butters, cooked eggs, fatty fish	Breast milk, infant formula, fish, poultry, DHA-fortified milk, eggs

Bottom line: Consciously include healthy sources of fat in your baby's diet as he moves through the first year. Fat should not be limited or restricted in infancy. Eating fish is a great way to get DHA and other healthy fats on board; start the fish eating habit early!

Calcium and vitamin D

Soft bones harden over time with a diet containing good sources of calcium and vitamin D, and weight-bearing exercises (pulling to stand, walking, running).

You'll want to include foods containing calcium and vitamin D, such as milk, later in the first year of life. Up until then, breast milk and a vitamin D supplement will cover requirements, as will infant formula.

Bottom line: Although you may be supplying a vitamin D supplement, it is good practice to include regular dairy products and fortified foods to cover these nutrients when it's age-appropriate to include them in your baby's diet (see Chapter xx). Your baby will need calcium and vitamin D his entire childhood, so start the habit of including them early.

Fiber and Other Nutrients

Most babies get the lion share of fiber from fruits, vegetables and grains. Fruits and vegetables also supply potassium, vitamin C, vitamin A, and other nutrients. Likewise, grains host the B complex vitamins, folate, magnesium, and other important nutrients for your baby.

Bottom Line: A well-rounded and balanced diet, including all food groups will ensure your baby gets the nutrients he needs. Work toward this goal as you move through the first year and advance solid foods.

6

Feeding Your Baby Matters

Believe it or not, starting solids includes more than the foods you introduce to your baby. *How* you go about feeding your baby is important, too. So much so, we now know that your feeding style and your feeding practices have a lot to do with whether your baby grows up to have a good relationship with food, likes a variety of foods, and is a healthy eater.

Responsive Feeding and The Trust Model

Your attentiveness and connection during the process of feeding your baby—or what is called responsive feeding-- sets the basis for HOW you feed her. Do you connect with your baby when feeding her by looking her in the eye or mimicking her sounds, or, are you multi-tasking and distracted by something else?

During infancy, establishing connection, trust, and promoting self-regulation are fundamental to healthy eating. The real power lies in combining WHAT and HOW you feed your child.

Responsive feeding is the lingo in infant nutrition describing the back and forth relationship between a parent and child that exists around feeding. Specifically, responsive feeding is characterized by the child's signals of hunger or fullness and the parent's responsiveness to those cues.

For example, your baby cries and seems to be hungry. You feed her. She pulls away from the nipple, and you end the feeding. This is responsive feeding at its core: your baby gives you an appetite sign and you respond appropriately to it.

Non-responsive feeding is the opposite. It goes something like this: your baby cries, seems to be hungry, but you hold her off because it isn't time to eat yet. And, when it is time, she eats but then pulls off the bottle after drinking most of it, but you want her to finish it, so you keep pushing it into her mouth.

Responsive feeding sets up the trust foundation between you and your child. Believe it or not, trust is anchored early on in childhood and feeding is one way it is established.

The trust you establish through feeding is a security blanket for your future interactions with your child around food and feeding. It carries over into toddlerhood and beyond. A baby who learns to trust that her caregiver will respond to her hunger and fullness may be more willing to follow your lead when you set up a schedule for meals and snacks, and when you say no to extra eating.

Researchers are finding that when responsive feeding is used in infancy and beyond, children are better at self-regulating their food intake and eating more food variety. These may contribute to a healthy body weight.

On the flip side, researchers also see that when non-responsive feeding is used, children are less good at self-regulating their appetite and eating (they don't listen to their body signals as well and may struggle with overeating or undereating), and this may contribute to weight problems, such as obesity.

Your Feeding Style

Did you know you have a feeding style? Much like a parenting style, you likely inherited your feeding style from your childhood upbringing. Feeding styles are the attitudes you use in the process of feeding your child and they closely mirror your parenting style.

Of course, if this is your first baby, it's hard to know or even recognize your feeding style. Regardless, it's important stuff in the raising of healthy eaters and I thought you'd like a little prelude into the next few years. If anything will test-drive your feeding style, it's the picky eating years between ages 2 and 6.

While one feeding style is generally the predominant one, a parent can find himself resorting to each feeding style, depending on the situation.

Let's review the different feeding styles:

Controlled feeding style is also known as a "parent-centered" feeding style. It may be associated with the "clean plate club," where rules about eating are emphasized, from trying foods to completing a meal. Dessert may be contingent upon eating dinner. Parents tend to plate food for their children, and eating is directed by the parent, rather than self-regulated by the child. A child may become resistant to trying new food, be picky, or an over-eater. Weight problems, both underweight and overweight, are correlated with this feeding style.

Indulgent feeding style is also known as "the lax parent," and reflects a child-directed feeding style. Even though the parent says "no" or a limitation may be the first response, "yes" ultimately wins. Children of permissive feeders may become overweight, as research shows that the limits on calorie-dense foods may be weak or non-existent.

Uninvolved feeding style often highlights the unprepared parent: irregular shopping, empty cabinets and refrigerators, and no plan for meals. Food and eating may lack importance for the parent, and that may transcend to feeding their child. Children who experience this feeding style may feel insecure and unsure about when they will have their next meal, whether they will like it, and if it will be enough. These children may become overly focused on food and frequently question the details around mealtime.

Authoritative feeding style is the "love with limits" feeding style, promoting independent thinking and self-regulation within the child, but also setting boundaries around food and eating. The authoritative feeder determines the details around the meal (what will be served, when it will happen, and where it will be served), but allows the child to decide whether they will eat what is prepared, and how much they will eat. This is essentially the definition of Satter's Division of Responsibility, which is a positive way to feed children. Trust and boundaries are the basis of this feeding style.

Children who have authoritative parents in the home tend to be leaner, good at self-regulating their food consumption, and feel secure with food and eating. The most current research advocates this style of feeding as an effective childhood obesity prevention approach.

Your Feeding Practices

The feeding styles we just reviewed are the foundation for the actions parents take when feeding their children. Meaning, how you feed your baby, or the actions you take and the tactics you employ reflect your feeding style.

Where feeding styles are the attitudes and beliefs, feeding practices are the day-to-day actions.

Feeding styles and practices are not linear, however. The research tells us that even though parents might have an inclination toward certain practices, the reaction and interaction with their child *also* informs how they feed. In other words, a parent influences a child's eating, but the child also influences a parent's feeding.

The toddler years are when feeding practices really show up. Here, I'm giving you a prequel of what to be aware of as you enter toddlerhood with your baby.

Pressure to Eat

Pressuring your child to eat takes many forms: nagging her to eat more, demanding a specified number of bites, mandating a trial of a new food, and reminding your child to eat or drink. Pressuring kids to eat is a sign of an authoritarian feeding style and, according to the research, may lead to disinterest in food, worsening of picky eating, early fullness, and poor weight gain, especially in the picky eater. Pressure to eat can have the opposite effect, too, potentially leading to overeating, poor food self-regulation and weight gain.

Rewards for Eating

Using sweets, dessert or other food incentives to get children to eat is called rewarding. Typically, rewarding is used to get children to eat certain foods like vegetables or to mold their behavior. Rewarding with food can get children to try new food or eat food they don't like, but there are long-term effects to consider. Research shows that kids who are rewarded with food learn that the reward food (dessert) is more valuable than the target food (oftentimes a vegetable). In other words, your child learns to value dessert over something healthy like a vegetable.

Catering to Food Preferences

When your child starts to become picky, you might get nervous about whether your child is getting enough nutrition. In addition to pressuring your child to eat and offering food rewards to motivate eating, you might be tempted to cater to your child's food preferences. In other words, you might fall into the trap of making what your child *will* eat, rather than the variety and array of foods you know is best for her. Studies show that parents who become short-order cooks have children with limited diets and who are less likely to try new foods and expand their diet.

Common Mistakes to Avoid

You might wonder why I went into these details in this starting solids book...

I do so to prepare you for the future! One thing I know from working with parents is that the feeding stages in the first year and beyond go *really* fast, and you have to be on your toes! Consider yourself prepared.

Section Three

Let's Start Solids!

Is this the moment you've been waiting for? Maybe. Or maybe not.

If you've made it this far, you are well-informed about the fundamental ideas behind being a smart mom who is starting solids with her baby. If you're still feeling scared or ambivalent about the process, then let's make sure your confidence is even higher. That's what this section is all about—giving you more knowledge to master this important stage in your baby's life.

In this section, I outline the different feeding methods you can use with feeding your baby, some rules to follow and the myriad food decisions you need to make, including food groups and food balance.

In Chapter 7, we discuss choosing the right feeding method for you and your baby, including spoon-feeding, baby-led weaning, or a combination of both. Chapter 8 details some of the food rules you need to be mindful of as you begin solid food, such as foods that cause choking and my sweets policy for babies. Last, in Chapter 9, we go over making baby food, whether and why to go conventional or organic in your baby food choices, and an introduction to the different food groups and how to strike a healthy balanced diet for your baby.

Let's start solids!

7

Choosing the Right Feeding Method

One thing I know from many, many years of working in the field of pediatric nutrition is that there isn't a right or wrong feeding method to use for your baby. So, don't let anyone pressure you into thinking there's one way to start solids.

It just isn't so.

There are three main feeding methods: spoon-feeding, baby-led weaning/self-feeding, and a combination of both.

Let's go through each method, so you have a better idea of which might work best for you and your baby:

Traditional: Spoon-Feeding Method

The spoon-feeding method has been around for a very long time. For almost fifty years, pureed baby food and iron-fortified infant cereal have been the recommended first foods. In fact, I was spoon-fed, and I'm betting you may have been, too!

While the conventional spoon-feeding method begins with a thin puree of iron-fortified baby cereal, it doesn't take your baby long to figure out how to manipulate food, chew and swallow.

Your baby will quickly move onto thicker consistencies of cereal and begin to eat single ingredient foods such as vegetables, fruit and other grains. Eventually, she will eat pureed meat, combination foods (meat, veggie, rice) and lumpier foods. This puree transition is quick and happens during the first month or two of eating solids.

The next step, the progression from pureed food to finger food, occurs at a predictable, yet individualized, pace. In general, around six to eight months of age, your baby will be ready to try soft, dissolvable finger foods such as crackers, small pieces of soft fruit and cooked vegetable, and tender meats in small pieces. He may still eat pureed food while exploring more solid, finger food textures.

Here's a general outline of how textures progress through the second 6 months with spoon feeding:

4-6 months:

Watery → Smooth, pureed, single ingredient foods

First foods may include the following:

- ✓ Baby cereal mixed with breastmilk or infant formula

- ✓ Single ingredient vegetables such as green bean, squash or carrots

- ✓ Single ingredient fruits such as banana, pear, or applesauce

- ✓ New research is suggesting a quick move to combinations of single ingredient foods to reduce pickiness later and increase liking of a variety of foods

6-8 months:

Pureed, single ingredient foods → Mashed or lumpy textures

You can combine single ingredient foods that your baby has tolerated (see above reason)

Soft, dissolvable finger foods

These foods include:

- ✓ Fork-mashed banana, avocado, or sweet potato
- ✓ Combinations of baby food previously eaten
- ✓ "Puffs," buttery crackers, buttered toast (lightly toasted) cut into "fingers"

8-10 months:

Mashed or lumpy foods → Chopped table foods

Chopped table foods might include the following:

- ✓ Chopped, cooked fruits and vegetables (canned fruit in water works well also)
- ✓ Soft cheeses (not made from raw milk)
- ✓ Mashed, cooked beans, and tofu
- ✓ Bread, toast, soft tortilla strips, crackers, dry cereal
- ✓ Well-cooked pasta
- ✓ Shredded, tender meats

10-12 months:

Chopped table foods → Chopped family food plus practice using a spoon

Chopped family food may include:

- ✓ Fresh, chopped fruit like bananas, grated apple without the skin
- ✓ Cooked vegetables
- ✓ Soft, chopped cooked meats and fish
- ✓ Cooked eggs

✓ Mixed dishes like casseroles

Words of Advice

Not all babies flow through this nice and neat texture progression. Some babies jump right to chopped foods while others march along through each of the stages of texture modifications in the outlined intervals.

Don't be alarmed if your baby doesn't follow this progression to a tee. Stage 3 baby food can be very challenging for your baby, as the combination of smooth and lumpy together may cause sensory confusion, and may result in gagging and choking. A baby who gags and chokes when eating may run the risk of a negative association, which can curtail eating progression later.

It's important that you are paying attention to your baby's signs of fullness if you are spoon-feeding. It's easy to fall into the "overfeeding" trap. If your baby is finished eating and showing you the signals of being done, don't force her to finish the jar of food or bowl of cereal. Honor her appetite cues, as this will help her eat the right amounts of food for her body, and not overeat.

New Age: Baby-Led Weaning

There is a trend of skipping pureed food altogether and diving right into family food. In this scenario, referred to as Baby-Led Weaning, food is modified so your baby can hold it and feed himself.

The term Baby-Led Weaning can be confusing, but don't let it be. This feeding approach got started in the UK where the term "weaning" means to start solid foods. In contrast, in the US, the term "weaning" means to transition off breast milk. Hence, the confusion! Just to be clear, if you are breastfeeding, you will continue to do so with this feeding approach.

Baby-led weaning has two phases: the first phase is devoted to exclusive breastfeeding during the first six months of life; the second phase is from six months on when baby begins solid food.

Six months is the minimum age to start solids, but age alone isn't the only criteria. In line with general recommendations to begin solids, developmental readiness to self-feed must be evident. During this second phase, baby is introduced to whole, unmodified food the family eats, offered in graspable pieces.

Researchers in Baby-Led Weaning define it as such:

Exclusive breast feeding for 6 months prior to offering finger foods from 6 months on, ninety percent of the time. Spoon-feeding and pureed food is used less than ten percent of the time.

At 6 months, baby feeds himself with hand-held, graspable pieces of food the whole family is eating. For example, a variety of food may be offered like fruits (avocado, banana), vegetables (cooked until soft), soft meats, cheese, well-cooked eggs, breads or toast, pasta and most fish.

Baby is brought to the table and presented with food the family eats, making eating a social occasion where baby learns from family members, and self-feeding happens more leisurely. Letting baby spontaneously start or "lead the way" with self-feeding may make the transition to solid food more rewarding for both baby and parent.

This approach has been studied, but there isn't a large body of evidence behind it-- yet. From what we know at the time of this writing, researchers suggest baby-led weaning encourages self-regulation, less pickiness, development of feeding skills, and leaner babies.

Some research suggests that lower calorie foods such as fruit and vegetables are more common in this feeding approach, which may be associated with a lower weight status in baby-led weaning babies compared to spoon-fed babies.

As Mother Nature would have it, some babies will fall outside of the six-month recommendation for beginning BLW. Some may be ready to start solids earlier than 6 months, and some may be simply late to self-feed. Baby Led Weaning doesn't allow manipulation of the texture of food to match your baby's development.

Additionally, children at this age do not have teeth for grinding complex textures or the tongue, lip, jaw and cheek coordination to chew and swallow food safely. They are in the process of learning these oral motor skills and the coordinated efforts of eating. In doing so, feeding sessions must be supervised. It's not uncommon for babies to gag when they start Baby-Led Weaning, and this can be concerning for parents. Always be present when your baby is eating, and assess whether the eating experience is a positive one. If your baby is gagging with each feeding session, it may be time to re-assess your feeding method.

The lack of eating skills may also make it difficult to meet the high nutrient needs (such as iron and zinc) of your baby. Babies who mostly self-feed, particularly in the early stages of BLW, may not receive adequate nutrients.

While this approach may seem scary (and risky), the safety net lies in education. Those parents who pay attention to food selection and choking hazards seem to do better by their baby with this feeding method.

One pilot study out of New Zealand looked at the impact of educating parents about BLW before they got started with their baby. Parents who were educated about iron, calorie density of foods, and choking hazards offered their babies high iron foods, which resulted in more iron consumed, though this was not statistically significant from the control group who weren't educated. They also gave their babies higher calorie foods and steered clear (mostly) of choking hazards.

Babies of BLW-educated parents also introduced more food variety to their babies than those who approached BLW without special instruction.

If you choose to use a Baby-Led Weaning approach for your baby, make sure to offer the important nutrient-rich foods we discussed in Chapter Five and be present and attentive during feeding sessions.

Also, I highly recommend the new book, *Born to Eat*, as required reading before you embark on Baby-Led Weaning.

The Middle Ground: Spoon & BLW

Another way to feed your baby is to allow him to use both baby-led weaning principles *and* the spoon. In my opinion, it's the best of both worlds.

Self-feeding is a term that encompasses a baby-led approach with food. For example, your baby may use his pincer grasp to pick up cereal or chunks of ripe banana and feed it to himself. He may hold a piece of tender steak and suck on it. Or, he may grab the spoon along with you and direct it to his mouth.

By using a combined approach of both self-feeding and spoon-feeding, your baby sets her own pace of eating, feeds herself, while getting important nutrients and calories that may be missed with a strictly BLW approach.

If you're feeling that you might be missing the mark with iron (it's hard for young babies to consume iron-rich foods like meat and beans), be sure to use an iron supplement to cover your baby's needs. You can also do a blend of BLW and spoon-feeding, making sure that what is on the spoon is iron-rich, like an iron-fortified mixed grain cereal or pureed meat.

Remember, the spoon is not a bad thing—your baby will eventually need to learn how to use it!

Take-Away:

The combo approach allows you to optimize the benefits of self-feeding and self-regulation, while assuring adequate nutrition, especially for iron, is consumed.

Common Feeding Mistakes

Here are some common mistakes I see parents make when feeding their baby:

Feeding Baby Separately from the Family

Separating your baby from the family meal experience may seem efficient, but a sacrifice is made: your baby's learning. Your baby learns by watching others eat. She learns about food variety and texture, and experiences eating as a social endeavor at the family table. Feeding your baby at separate times and in a separate place denies her this learning experience.

Pull the highchair up to the family table as soon and as frequently as possible, ideally before the end of the first year, whether you are spoon-feeding, following BLW, or doing a combination of both.

Avoiding the Mess of Eating

Feeding your baby is a messy job. You wipe his face after a couple of bites, clean his tray periodically, and spoon-feed him to avoid the mess. But, the real magic of learning about and liking food takes place when your baby is interacting with food: touching, smelling, smearing, tasting and playing with it.

Don't distract your baby while he's eating. Let him experience food uninterrupted.

Getting Caught Up in the Latest Feeding Approaches (and Forgetting Nutrition)

I see many well-intentioned parents get caught up in the latest feeding approaches. The choice of feeding approach isn't the mistake. The mistake lies in being unprepared to match your baby's needs for important nutrients or being so invested in a certain method, you fail to see it isn't a good fit for *your* child.

Unfortunately, I have seen babies in my practice who are underweight/Failure to Thrive and who have iron-deficiency anemia. These nutritional repercussions stem from a lack of food and nutrients for their baby. I've seen babies who aren't doing well with BLW, gagging with feedings, and who fare better with a combined approach of spoon and self-feeding. I've also seen babies who are overfed with the spoon. Bottom Line: Learn about the essential components for success with each feeding method and make a change if needed.

My Advice:

Whatever feeding method you choose, be sure to do your homework and match your baby's nutritional needs. Don't persist with a method that isn't working for your baby, but be open and flexible to finding a feeding approach that ensures your baby thrives—physically, developmentally and emotionally.

8

Rules for First Foods

Starting the journey of first foods can be stressful for any parent, but it shouldn't be. Not after you understand how to do it, and how to side step the hazards. In this chapter, I lay out the obvious scenarios that can get in the way of a successful experience with starting solids.

Prevent Choking

Approximately 40 percent of fatal choking incidents and 60 percent of nonfatal choking episodes in children are associated with food items. Candy and chewing gum are the foods most often implicated.

The best way to avoid a choking incident is to supervise your baby, use small portions, steer clear of known choking hazards, and keep a calm atmosphere during feeding sessions.

The following food characteristics may be problematic for your baby:

Size – Both small and large pieces of food may cause choking. Small hard pieces of food (such as nuts and seeds, or small pieces of raw hard vegetables) may get into the airway if they are swallowed before being chewed properly. Larger pieces may be more difficult to chew and are more likely to completely block a baby's airway if inhaled.

Shape – Food items shaped like a sphere or cylinder may cause choking because they are likely to block the airway more completely

THE SMART MOM'S GUIDE TO STARTING SOLIDS

than other shapes. Some examples are whole grapes, hot dog-shaped products (including meat sticks and string cheese), and round candies.

Consistency – Foods that are firm, smooth, or slick may slip down the throat. Some examples are whole grapes; nuts; hard candy; hot dog-like products; string cheese; large pieces of fruit with skin; fruit with membranes, like clementines; whole pieces of canned fruit; and raw peas.

Dry or hard foods may be difficult to chew and easy to swallow whole. Some examples are popcorn, nuts and seeds, small hard pieces of raw vegetable, cookies, pretzels, and potato chips. Sticky or tough foods (e.g., peanut butter, dried fruit, tough meat, sticky candy) may not break apart easily and may be hard to remove from the airway.

Never leave your baby alone while he's eating and never rely on another child (ie, sibling) to monitor your baby when eating.

Feed to Prevent Food Allergies

We cannot predict which children will develop a food allergy and which ones will not. However, experts believe that those children with a strong family history of food allergy, allergy to pollen, mold or other elements, asthma, and atopic dermatitis are at a higher risk for developing a food allergy. These children have a genetic or inherited tendency to acquire a food allergy.

Early introduction of solid food (before 4 months of age) is associated with a higher risk for developing a food allergy. Remember, at this young age, your baby's digestive system isn't fully mature, making it more susceptible to alerting the immune system against food allergens.

In countries like the United States and the United Kingdom, the practice has been to restrict food allergens in the first few years of life. However, in foreign countries like Israel, peanuts are introduced before 9 months of age, and children have a lower incidence of peanut allergy.

Recent research out of the UK and recommendations from the American Academy of Pediatrics have changed to reflect the current research. It is now advised to *allow* food allergens, like milk, soy, egg, peanut, tree nuts, fish and wheat, age-appropriately, between ages 6 and 12 months.

One way to make this happen is to introduce solids around age 6 months, initially using single ingredient foods such as iron-fortified infant cereal, pureed fruit, vegetable and meats offered every two to three days.

Watch for signs of intolerance like spitting up or vomiting, diarrhea, or skin rashes, which may indicate an allergic reaction. If no negative reaction is seen, proceed with the next new food.

Make sure to incorporate the known allergens in your baby's diet as you move through the third and fourth quarter of your baby's first year of life. For example, work in cooked egg, salmon, bread, and peanut butter. More on this later.

Portion Sizes: Do They Matter?

Yes, there are recommended portions for your baby. These are mostly outlined so you will have a notion of how much food to give your baby at meals and snacks, and which foods to provide so you strike an ideal food balance that reflects and matches your baby's nutritional needs.

I think the best way to use portions is to let them guide you with how much food to start with. After that, I believe it's best to let your baby lead with his instinctive appetite.

Here are the recommended starting portions for your baby:

Food Group	Amount (8-12 months)	Servings per day
Protein (meat, chicken, turkey, fish, cooked beans)	3-4 Tablespoons	2
Egg	1	
Grains Baby cereal Bread, crackers	2-4 Tablespoons ¼ slice, 2	2-3
Fruit	3-4 Tablespoons	2
Vegetables	3-4 Tablespoons	2
Dairy Infant Formula Breastmilk Cheese Yogurt Cottage Cheese	6-8 ounces on demand ½ ounce ½ cup ¼ cup	3-4 offer

Watch Out for Sweets

A sip of mom's latte and a nibble of cookie may seem harmless, but it can influence your baby's future food preferences, eating habits and health. With limited tummy space and high nutrient needs, babies have no room for sweets in their diet. Accordingly, the American Heart Association (AHA) recommends no added sugar during the first two years.

Try to minimize commercially prepared infant food desserts, commercial cakes, cookies, candies, and sweet pastries in the first two years of life. Watch out for chocolate, as some infants have hypersensitivity (allergic) reactions to it.

Avoid honey under 12 months of age. It can cause infant botulism which can lead to death. Even cooked foods with honey may have live spores and a baby's GI tract is not equipped to destroy the spores on his or her own.

What About Water?

Breast milk or infant formula are the *only* beverages that should be offered to infants less than 6 months of age. Thereafter, a small amount of water (~4 to 8 ounces per day) in a cup is okay to offer around the time when complementary foods are introduced.

9:

Your Best Food Options

This chapter is all about food. I know you've been waiting for this! By now, you know when to recognize when your baby is ready to start solids, which nutrients to pay attention to, and which feeding method with which you want to begin. Now it's time to talk about how to choose a nutrient-rich diet for your growing baby.

First, I will cover the pros and cons of commercial versus homemade baby food and whether you should opt for organic or conventional foods. Then, for ease, and to prepare you for what lies ahead, I will categorize food for your baby into food groups: Grains, fruits and vegetables, and protein. I'll touch a bit on dairy, especially as it pertains to offering dairy products like cheese, but during this first year your baby's dairy requirements will be met by breastmilk or formula.

Commercial or Homemade Baby Food?

This is one of the main questions parents have as the embark on starting solids with their baby...

Should I buy jarred or pouched food, or should I make homemade baby food?

Honestly, there are pros and cons for each, and it really boils down to your personal situation and your preferences.

Homemade is fresher and gives you the option to introduce spices and herbs to increase flavor variability (see the herb and spice chart in the Appendix for ideas) as well as vary the consistency and texture.

Commercial baby food has been revolutionized recently. Using a pasteurization method that relies on cold rather than heat processing, commercial baby food is fresher than ever before and is touting unique foods and flavor combinations.

Either route you choose, remember, it doesn't have to be an exclusive method. You can do both! Mash a ripe banana and mix into baby cereal; puree some slow cooker beef in broth, mash an avocado and offer a pureed peaches and mango pouch (on a spoon).

Organic or Conventional Food?

There is evidence that children who consume organic fruits and vegetables have lower pesticide levels in their urine than children who eat conventional sources. Children are at the greatest risk for adverse effects on the brain due to pesticide exposure because their brain is still developing and their exposure is greater, pound for pound.

If you can, purchase organic fruits and vegetables that are known to have lower levels of pesticide exposure. The Environmental Working Group (EWG) has a dirty dozen list that comes out each year, which you can find on their website. At the time of this writing (2017), the following are the fruits and vegetables with the highest pesticide content:

- ✓ **Fruits**: strawberries, nectarines, apples, peaches, pears, cherries, grapes

- ✓ **Vegetables**: spinach, celery, tomatoes, sweet bell pepper, potatoes, hot peppers

If these organic fruits and vegetables are not a possibility for your family, don't worry! It's far more important that your baby is exposed to a variety of fruits and vegetables, in any form (frozen, canned, etc), so that he can experience the flavors and health benefits of these foods and learn to like them. Be sure to wash all produce, whether organic or not!

Food Groups: Grains

As you've learned, fortified infant cereal has been and continues to be a good first food choice for your baby. It is iron-rich (and sometime rich in zinc also), easy to digest, is unlikely to cause an allergic reaction, and you can alter its texture (from soupy and thin to dense and lumpy) to help your baby move along in her eating skills.

Iron-fortified rice, oat, barley and mixed grains are good options. Reconstitute these cereals with breast-milk or formula.

Initially, avoid ready-to-eat cereals (boxed cereals for older kids) until your baby is older. They contain mixed grains, are higher in salt and sugar, and provide less iron per serving than baby cereal. Also, these may contain nuts or dried fruit, which may cause choking.

Best Practice:

Choose infant cereals and rotate the different kinds to minimize the exposure to arsenic.

Around 6 to 8 months, many infants are ready to try crackers, bread, noodles, macaroni, and other grain products. By this stage in their development, infants can practice picking up these foods with their fingers.

Try: Plain ground or mashed rice or barley; chopped noodles; plain enriched or whole grain crackers, preferably low in salt; small pieces of toast or crust of bread; and zwieback, teething biscuits, or graham crackers

Best practice:

Cook noodles until very soft. It is best to mash or finely chop (1/2-inch pieces or smaller) cooked noodles, spaghetti, and macaroni until the infant is 8 to 10 months or older.

Food Groups: Fruit and Vegetables

Fruits and vegetables provide infants with carbohydrates, including fiber, vitamins A and C, and minerals. The order of introduction, fruits first or vegetables first, is not important. However, you'll want to introduce a wide variety of vegetables and fruits over time (even if you don't like them yourself).

Plain vegetables and fruits generally offer more nutrient value for the price compared to fruit-based dessert combinations.

The AAP recommends that spinach, beets, turnips, carrots, or collard greens prepared at home, such as when making homemade baby food, should not be fed to infants under 6 months old because they may contain sufficient nitrates to cause methemoglobinemia. Methemoglobinemia is a condition where nitrates react with hemoglobin in your baby's blood, ultimately starving your baby's blood of oxygen.

This is also called blue baby syndrome, and is characterized by blue skin and difficulty breathing and could lead to death. This only seems to be a risk when high-nitrate veggies are included in homemade baby food, and is generally a concern when babies are under 6 months of age. Commercially prepared infant and junior spinach, carrots, and beets contain only traces of nitrate and are not considered a risk to your baby.

Best Practice:

Do not to feed infants under 6 months any home-made baby food using vegetables with high nitrate content.

Avoid veggies that may cause a choking hazard such as:

- ✓ raw vegetables (including green peas, string beans, celery, carrot, etc.)
- ✓ cooked or raw whole corn kernels
- ✓ whole, uncut cherry or grape tomatoes

✓ hard pieces of raw fruit

✓ whole pieces of canned fruit

✓ whole, uncut grapes, berries, cherries, or melon balls (these fruits should be cut into quarters, with pits removed, before feeding)

✓ uncooked dried fruit (including raisins)

Don't Let Fruits and Veggies Take a Nose Dive

Studies show that infants experience a significant drop in fruit and vegetable intake at 9 months, and as a result, other common snacks such as cereal, cookies, crackers and French fries are eaten instead. French fries are the number one "vegetable" for toddlers!

This is an unfortunate fact and is the foundation for our nation's children getting behind in nutrition and important nutrients as they grow up. Be sure to keep fruits and vegetables in the menu plan ... even if your baby is refusing to eat them. Exposure to the foods you want your child to eat is the key to eventually accepting them again.

Food Groups: Protein

Protein-rich foods are generally introduced to infants between 6 and 8 months of age. However, if your baby is developmentally ready and needs a good source of iron and zinc (ie, exclusively breast fed), then introduce it around 6 months.

Protein-rich foods include meat, poultry, fish, egg yolks, cheese, yogurt, and legumes.

Best Practice:

Infants can be offered well-cooked strained or pureed lean beef, pork, lamb, veal, chicken, turkey, liver, boneless finfish (fish other than shellfish), cooked egg yolk and whole egg, legumes, tofu, sliced or grated mild cheese, yogurt, or cottage cheese.

Introduce fish in the first year of life, choosing those fish sources that are lower in mercury, per the Food and Drug Administration (FDA) and the Environmental Protection Agency (EPA). See the Appendix for a listing of low mercury fish.

Commercially prepared plain baby food meats offer more nutrients than mixed dinners.

Make your own combined "dinners" by combining baby cereal, meat and veggie or fruit.

Eggs

Cooked eggs can be introduced to infants in the first year (even as early as 6 months as it is linked to protection from food allergy development). Start with the cooked egg yolk, then advance to the whole egg.

Raw eggs should never be fed to your baby (or anyone else) because they may contain bacteria that can cause illness.

Dairy Foods

Cottage cheese, hard cheeses, and yogurt can be offered as protein foods after 8 months. Since these foods contain similar proteins to cow's milk, infants should be observed closely for reactions after eating them.

Cheese can be eaten cooked in foods or in the sliced form. Small slices or strips of cheese are easier and safer to eat than a chunk of cheese, which could cause choking.

Beans and Legumes

Cooked legumes (dry beans and peas) or tofu (bean curd made from soybeans) can be introduced into an infant's diet as a protein food, but may need to be mashed or cooked to a softer consistency for your baby. Introduce small quantities (1 to 2 teaspoons) of mashed or pureed and strained legumes initially to avoid choking.

Nuts

Nuts, in general, are a choking hazard for infants and should not be offered. However, the latest guidelines for infants support the introduction of peanut products around 6 months of age to prevent the development of peanut allergy.

Best practice:

To work in peanuts into your baby's diet, offer peanut products such as peanut butter, peanut flour or peanut puffs (Bamba) to baby in a developmentally appropriate manner, like mixed into baby cereal or oatmeal. Use a thin spread of peanut butter on bread or mix peanut flour into pancake batter or muffin mix.

Juice?

About eighty percent of 6 to 9 month old infants drink juice regularly. This may program your infant to like and prefer sugary, sweet flavors, and may contribute to excess weight.

The other problem with fruit juice is that it can crowd out important nutrients. Fruit juice is filling, and can cause gastrointestinal symptoms, such as diarrhea, abdominal pain, or bloating. Certain juices are more problematic for baby and toddler, especially those containing a significant amount of sorbitol, a naturally occurring carbohydrate.

Juices containing sorbitol include prune, pear, cherry, peach, and apple juice.

The AAP has concluded that fruit juice offers no nutritional benefit for infants less than 6 months and no benefit over whole fruits for infants older than 6 months.

Best Practice:

Currently, the AAP recommends no juice for babies under one year of age, stating that it has no nutritional benefits for this age group. After your baby is a year old, never feed your baby unpasteurized juice.

Don't offer fruit juice at nap or bedtime in a bottle as it is associated with a higher risk for dental caries.

Section Four

Staying on Track Through the First Year

Last, but not least, let's put all this food information together. In Chapter 10, I give you more details on food advancement schedules, why there's a waiting period between new foods, and what it looks like to feed your baby during a day with some sample meal plans at each transitional stage. In Chapter 11, it's all about your baby's next steps, including using a cup, setting up a structure for your day to day feeding, and bringing your baby to the family table.

10

Ready, Set, Advance!

In many ways, getting ready to start your baby on solids is like taking a trip. You need to plan, get a lay of the land, map out your excursion, and start driving. That's exactly what you've been doing in this book—mapping your excursion in the first year of life as it relates to feeding your baby.

I could have given you the foods, portions and schedule up front, but there's a madness to my method. (Yes, I know that's stated backwards...)

I am keen on preparing you with a comprehensive guidebook for starting your baby on solids, the right way. If you know me at all, you know I believe we nourish our children best when we nourish them completely and holistically. Hence, the previous chapters laying the groundwork of feeding and all the choices you need to think about before you begin.

So, in this chapter, you'll get the goods. You will learn why there is a waiting period between new foods. You'll get a chart outlining a month by month progression of food, and you'll get a sample day menu plan for each age transition.

What's Behind the Waiting Period?

Waiting between introducing new foods to your baby allows you to observe any negative reactions to food that may occur. You'll also be better able to pinpoint which food caused the reaction.

An adverse reaction may include gagging, choking, or signs of an allergic response (vomiting, diarrhea, rash, wheezing, anaphylaxis).

As I discussed, the AAP no longer asks parents to wait on introducing certain foods to prevent food allergies. Furthermore, the waiting period of 3 to 5 days between foods is an arbitrary recommendation, based more on tradition than science.

When you think about the goal of exposing your baby to a wide variety of different foods in the first year of life, waiting 3 to 5 days means he only sees a new food twice a week. And, if you crunch the numbers, your baby will only see 6 to 10 new foods a month! In my opinion, this is not enough food exposure to create an adventurous eater.

Best Practice:

If your baby shows good tolerance after 1 to 3 days of having a new food, move on to the next food and start mixing tolerated foods together in unique combinations.

Month-by-Month Food Introduction Guide Using the Spoon

If you are spoon-feeding your baby, I've pulled together all the recommendations I covered earlier into one handy chart. If you are using a BLW feeding method, you'll be less concerned with food transitions, but this chart, and the following menus, may inspire some food and meal planning strategies for you.

Month-by-Month Food Introduction Guide

	4 to 6 months	6 to 8 months	8 to 10 months	10 to 12 months
Grains	Iron-fortified whole grain cereal like oats	Mixed grain cereal; soft, dissolvable crackers and finger foods	Unsweetened ready-to-eat cereals, small and soft pieces bread, cooked pasta	All grains
Fruit	Pureed apples, pears; ripe banana, avocado	Mild, raw, ripe fruits: pears, peach, cantaloupe, mango	Chopped: strawberries, blueberries, grated apple	Chopped: orange, clementine; quartered (or more) grapes
Vegetables	Pureed sweet potato, green beans, peas	Soft cooked and/or fork mashed: Carrots, potatoes, squash, broccoli	Chopped: Beets, spinach, kale	Tomatoes, chopped lettuce, all veggies
Protein	Pureed: Beef, turkey, chicken	Mashed: Fish, egg, tofu, beans, peanut products	Chopped: Mixed meals	All kinds
Dairy		Full fat yogurt (cow or soy)	Natural cheeses	

Sample Menus Based on Your Baby's Age

The day in the life of your baby will look dramatically different as he or she grows in the first year. For one, when your baby starts solids, he will barely be getting any food, and will still be very reliant on your breastmilk or formula. As you know by now, eating is a learning experience, rather than a nutritious endeavor.

Over the months, though, food will become a centerpiece of the day, with three meals and three snacks shaping it. The snacks may include at least one bottle or breast feeding session, but eventually will showcase food and a cup.

Did I tell you food and feeding happen in rapid-fire succession?!

I've outlined a sample day of eating for each stage of solid food progression so you have an idea of what your baby's day could look like. These menus are adapted from Fearless Feeding: How to Raise Healthy Eaters from High Chair to High School.

(I know many mommas who just want to have a reference point for comparison...these menus are in no way set in stone, but rather a representation of the rhythm and flow any day with your baby's eating could hold.)

Sample Day for a 4 to 6 month-old

Morning	Nursing or a bottle
Breakfast	1 to 2 Tbsp. baby cereal mixed with breastmilk or formula 1 to 2 Tbsp. pureed fruit or veggie
Mid-morning	Nursing or a bottle
Lunch	Nursing or a bottle
Afternoon	Nursing or a bottle
Dinner	1 to 2 Tbsp. cereal or meat 1 to 2 Tbsp. fruit or veggie Nursing or a bottle
Bedtime	Nursing or a bottle

Sample Menu for a 6 to 8 month-old

Morning	Nursing or a bottle
Breakfast	2 to 4 Tbsp. baby cereal mixed with breastmilk or formula 2 to 3 Tbsp. pureed fruit or veggie 1 egg mashed with formula or breastmilk
Mid-morning	Nursing or a bottle
Lunch	Nursing or a bottle
Afternoon	1 to 4 Tbsp. cereal mixed with formula or breastmilk (peanut flour mixed in) 2 to 3 Tbsp. fruit or veggie ½ cup yogurt
Dinner	2 to 3 Tbsp. meat or non-meat alternative 2 crackers (a serving of grain) 2 to 3 Tbsp. fruit or veggie Nursing or a bottle
Bedtime	Nursing or a bottle

Sample Menu for an 8 to 10 month-old

Morning	Nursing or a bottle
Breakfast	4 to 6 Tbsp. baby oats mixed with formula or breastmilk and peanut butter 2 to 4 Tbsp. pureed fruit or veggie 1 egg mashed with formula or breastmilk
mid-morning	Nursing or a bottle

Lunch	2 to 4 Tbsp. meat or non-meat alternative 3 to 4 Tbsp. pasta (serving of grain) 2 to 4 Tbsp. fruit or veggie Nursing or a bottle
Afternoon	2 to 4 Tbsp. fruit or veggie ½ cup yogurt
Dinner	2 to 4 Tbsp. meat or non-meat alternative ½ slice of bread (a serving of grain) 2 to 4 Tbsp. veggie Nursing or a bottle
Bedtime	Nursing or a bottle

Sample Menu for 10 to 12 month-old

Morning	Nursing or a bottle
Breakfast	Thin spread peanut butter on toast 1 scrambled egg chopped melon
mid-morning	Cut up banana Graham cracker
Lunch	½ grilled cheese sandwich ¼ cup cooked green beans Nurse or bottle
Afternoon	¼ cup blueberries ½ cup yogurt Nurse or bottle

Dinner	1 to 2 ounces chopped chicken ¼ cup baked sweet potato (mashed) ¼ cup applesauce water
Bedtime	Nurse or a bottle

As you can see in these menus, your baby's food intake gradually shifts to showcase less liquid nutrition and more food. I've also tried to show where and how you can incorporate peanut products and other allergens in your baby's diet. Remember, most babies, even those who are at a high risk for food allergy, can begin to eat food allergens in the first year. If you are uncertain whether your baby should proceed with allergens, consult with your doctor.

While you and your baby are in the "honeymoon phase" of feeding in the first year – a time when your baby will eat just about anything you serve him – this will not always be the case.

Read on for a head's up on your baby's year-end goals for eating and feeding!

11

Next Steps for the Next Year

Several things should be in place by the end of the first year. I call these your baby's End of the Year Goals. I think it's good to have a handle on these to help you stay on track and monitor your baby's feeding milestones. If your baby gets behind, you can quickly address it.

For one, your baby should be drinking out of a cup and transitioning away from the bottle (if you're breastfeeding, continue to do so for as long as you like). Your baby should be exploring food (or, playing with it) and using her self-feeding skills. She should be playing with or even using a spoon, and eating with you at the family table.

About that Cup

At about 6 months, most infants develop the ability to, with assistance, drink from a cup with some liquid escaping from their mouths. After 8 months, when infants begin to curve their lips around the rim of a cup, they're able to drink from a cup with less spilling.

Introduce small amounts (1 to 2 ounces) of infant formula, breast milk, or water in a "baby-sized" regular plastic cup. Hold the cup for your baby and feed her very slowly, tilting the cup so that a very small amount of liquid (one mouthful) leaves the cup. By doing so, your baby can swallow the liquids without hurry.

Cups with spill-proof lids (sippy cups with "stoppers") are not rec-ommended since they may encourage the infant to carry the cup and drink more often. They are also difficult to suck from and may impair your baby's normal oral muscle development. Rather, transition to a straw cup as it strengthens oral development, including speech.

Transitioning to a Structured Schedule

As you can see from the sample meal plans, your baby will gradual-ly transition from on demand feeding to eating with a structure to her meals and snacks during the first year. Regular meals and snacks help children get the myriad requirement of nutrients in their diet while helping keep their appetite on an even keel. In the young tod-dler, a structure provides many opportunities to eat and meet nutri-tional requirements, especially since their tummies are small. Young toddlers eat about every 2 to 3 hours.

As you move into a rhythm with meals and snacks, you'll want to add an element of routine to the process. For example, not only do meals and snacks have a regular time, they should also have a regular place, like in the kitchen or at the meal table. They should be distrac-tion-free, meaning no toys, TV or other distractions.

I cannot emphasize how important this transition to structured meals and snacks is for your baby turned toddler. Structure is the key to your continued support of your child's self-regulatory skills with eating.

As a reminder, let your baby take his time eating, and when he shows you he's done, let him be done. No need to extend the meal in hopes of more eating, or force-feeding to get more food into him. Let your baby lead the way with his pace of eating and amounts of food in-take. Remember, there are several opportunities for your baby to eat throughout the day!

Joining the Family Table

Last, your baby should make a regular appearance at the family meal table, even if it's just with you. The family table adds a social element to eating, as well as creating a time for uninterrupted connection. Watching others eat and learning the social dynamic of talking, eating, passing food, laughing and more teaches baby on a deep level what it means to gather together for a meal. I like to see all babies at the meal table by the end of the first year or earlier!

P.S. Make sure to always try to keep mealtime pleasant and the meal table a highlight of your child's day.

Conclusion

Although many parents who have babies are unsure about starting solids, you, my friend, are not a statistic any more. You are not one of the 54% of parents who are confused and scared about embarking on this transition with their baby.

You are a smart mom.

You have the information, knowledge and confidence to start your baby on solids in a timely, nutritious, and successful way. I wish I had this information packaged together when my babes were embarking on this important transition. I would have done a few things differently.

My hope for you is that you find your preferred feeding method, optimal food choices and food balance, and progress through the transition easily and without challenge.

But I also hope you put your heart and soul into the feeding and caring of your little one. That you pay attention to his nutrient needs, the connection you can establish through feeding, and summon the patience to let him lead the way with eating.

After all, a smart mom knows that feeding her baby is more than shoveling food into his mouth or following some new diet. Nourishing your baby is connecting through meals, loving food and transmitting that love to your child, supporting your baby's self-regulation with eating, and feeding his whole being, inside and out.

Resources:

Fearless Feeding: How to Raise Healthy Eaters from High Chair to High School by Jill Castle MS, RDN and Maryann Jacobsen, MS, RDN

The Calcium Handbook: Over 100 Ways to Build Healthy Bones in Your Child by Jill Castle

Try New Food: Help New Eaters, Picky Eaters & Extremely Picky Eaters Taste, Eat & Like New Food by Jill Castle

Feed Your Baby, Save Your Sanity online course by Clancy Harrison

Born to Eat: Whole Healthy Foods from Baby's First Bite by Wendy Jo Peterson and Leslie Schilling

Food Allergies Updated Guidelines from National Institute of Allergy and Infectious Diseases: https://www.nih.gov/news-events/news-releases/nih-sponsored-expert-panel-issues-clinical-guidelines-prevent-peanut-allergy

Child of Mine by Ellyn Satter

Appendix

Herb & Spice Flavoring Chart

HERB or SPICE	PAIR WITH
Sweet Basil	apricots, bell peppers (red), broccoli, blueberries, carrots, corn, peaches, peas, potatoes, rice, tomatoes, white beans, zucchini
Cilantro	avocado, bell pepper, coconut milk, corn, cucumber, rice, figs, yogurt, carrots, potatoes, soups, stews, root vegetables
Cinnamon	apples, almonds, apricots, bananas, blueberries, chicken, pears, pancakes, French toast, yogurt, oatmeal, rice
Cumin	apples, beans, beef, chickpeas, couscous, eggplants, lentils, potatoes, rice, sauerkraut, squash, tomatoes
Dill	asparagus, avocados, beets, cabbage, carrots, celery, cucumber, fish, potatoes, rice, salmon, tomatoes, yogurt, zucchini, cabbage, onion, pumpkin
Garlic	chicken, lamb, meats, tomatoes, vegetables, zucchini
Ginger	apples, chicken, fish, passion fruit, pears, pineapple, mango
Mint	asparagus, beans, baby carrots, cucumbers, eggplant, peas, potatoes, tomatoes, yogurt
Oregano	anchovies, artichokes, beans, bell peppers, cabbage, cauliflower, corn, chicken, eggplant, eggs, fish, lamb, meat, pizza, pork potatoes, sweet peppers, squash, tomatoes, zucchini

Rosemary	apricots, beans, bell peppers, cabbage, chicken, eggs, eggplant, fish, lentils, peas, pork, potatoes, soups, stews, tomatoes, winter squash
Tarragon	artichokes, asparagus, eggs, fish, potatoes, poultry, tomatoes, zucchini
Thyme	beans, cabbage, carrots, chicken, corn, eggplant, fish, lamb, meats, onions, potatoes, soups, stews, tomatoes, winter vegetables

Adapted from: Clancy Harrison's Food Herb & Spice Pairing Chart from Feeding Baby, Save Your Sanity

Food Sources of Vitamin C

Food	Portion Size	Vitamin C (mg)
Red pepper, sweet, raw	1/2 cup	158
Orange juice	3/4 cup	155
Orange	1 medium	117
Grapefruit juice	3/4 cup	117
Kiwifruit	1 medium	107
Green pepper, sweet, raw	1/2 cup	100
Broccoli, cooked	1/2 cup	85
Strawberries, fresh, sliced	1/2 cup	82
Brussels sprouts, cooked	1/2 cup	80
Vegetable juice cocktail	1 cup	67
Grapefruit	1/2 medium	65
Broccoli, raw	1/2 cup	65
Fortified ready-to-eat cereals (various)	3/4 - 1 1/3 cup (~1 ounce)	60-61
Tomato juice	3/4 cup	55
Cantaloupe	1/2 cup	48
Cabbage, cooked	1/2 cup	47

Papaya	1/2 cup	43
Cauliflower, raw	1/2 cup	43
Pineapple	1/2 cup	39
Potato, baked	1 medium	28
Tomato, raw	1 medium	28
Kale, cooked from fresh	1/2 cup	27
Tangerine	1 medium	24
Mango	1/2 cup	23
Spinach, cooked	1/2 cup	15
Green peas, frozen, cooked	1/2 cup	13

Adapted from *Fearless Feeding: How to Raise Healthy Eaters from High Chair to High School*

Easy Fork-Mashed Foods

Fork-mashed foods are ideal after the first smooth puree phase is over and your baby is ready for more texture.

Fruit

Ripe fruit mashes easily! Some fruit will need to be peeled and sliced before mashing.

✓ Banana

✓ Mango (peel and slice first)

✓ Cantaloupe

✓ Plum

✓ Bosc pear

✓ Papaya

✓ Fresh fig

✓ Apricot

✓ Peach (peel and slice first)

✓ Avocado

Vegetables

Most vegetables will have to be cooked first before fork-mashing.

- ✓ Baked potato
- ✓ Baked sweet potato
- ✓ Steamed squash
- ✓ Steamed peas
- ✓ Steamed zucchini
- ✓ Cooked carrots

Other Foods

If a food is dry, add breast milk or infant formula to moisten.

- ✓ Soft tofu
- ✓ Poached fish
- ✓ Ground chicken, turkey or beef (cook to well-done)
- ✓ Soft pasta or rice

Mercury Content of Fish

Fish offers your baby important nutrients, like healthy fats and DHA. Certain fish, however, may contain mercury in amounts that can harm your baby. Follow the chart below to choose low mercury fish.

Access the full chart here:

https://www.fda.gov/downloads/Food/FoodborneIllnessContaminants/Metals/UCM536321.pdf

Best Choices (eat 2-3 servings/ week)	Good Choices (eat 1 serving/week)	Avoid (highest mercury levels)
Anchovy	Bluefish	King Mackerel
Atlantic croaker	Buffalofish	Marlin
Atlantic mackerel	Carp	Orange roughy
Black sea bass	Chilean sea bass	Shark
Butterfish	Grouper	Swordfish
Catfish	Halibut	Tilefish (from Gulf of Mexico)
Clam	Mahi Mahi	Tuna (bigeye)
Cod	Monkfish	

Crab	Rockfish	
Crawfish	Sablefish	
Flounder	Sheepshead	
Haddock	Snapper	
Hake	Spanish mackerel	
Herring	Striped bass (ocean)	
Lobster, American and spiny	Tilefish (from Atlantic ocean)	
Mullet	Tuna, albacore/white tuna, canned and fresh/frozen	
Oyster	Tuna, yellowfin	
Pacific chub mackerel	Weakfish/seatrout	
Perch, freshwater and ocean	White croaker/Pacific croaker	
Pickerel		
Plaice		
Pollock		
Salmon		
Sardine		
Scallop		
Shad		
Shrimp		
Skate		
Smelt		
Sole		
Squid		
Tilapia		
Trout, freshwater		

Tuna,		
canned light (in-cludes skipjack)		
Whitefish		
Whiting		

Adapted from: Environmental Protection Agency and U.S. Food and Drug Administration

About the Author

Jill Castle has practiced as a registered dietitian/nutritionist in the field of pediatric nutrition for over 25 years. Formerly a clinical pediatric dietitian at Massachusetts General Hospital and Children's Hospital, Boston, Jill currently works as a private practitioner, online educator, consultant, and speaker.

She is the author of *Eat Like a Champion: Performance Nutrition for Your Young Athlete*, co-author of *Fearless Feeding: How to Raise Healthy Eaters from High Chair to High School*, creator of The Nourished Child, a childhood nutrition blog and podcast, and creator of The Nourished Child Project and Eat Like a Champion, online courses for parents and young athletes.

Jill has been published in peer-reviewed journals, textbooks, consumer books, cookbooks, websites, and other blogs. She is a national and international speaker, focused on topics related to childhood nutrition, including feeding, picky eating, youth sports nutrition, and childhood obesity.

Jill is regularly quoted in popular print and online publications as a leading childhood nutrition expert.

Jill lives in Connecticut with her husband, four children and two dogs. For more, go to www.JillCastle.com

Books Authored by Jill Castle

Fuel Up! Dinner Recipes for Young Athletes

Fast & Nutritious Breakfasts for Young Athletes

Nutrients for Kids, Advanced Guide

The Healthy Snack Planner for Kids

Try New Food: Help New Eaters, Picky Eaters, and Extremely Picky Eaters Taste, Eat & Like New Foods

The Calcium Handbook: Over 100 Ways to Grow Healthy Bones for Your Child

The Kids Healthy Weight Project Workbook

Eat Like a Champion: Performance Nutrition for Your Young Athlete

Fearless Feeding: How to Raise Healthy Eaters from High Chair to High School

Made in the USA
Monee, IL
26 February 2020